DISTINCTIVE DIFFERENCE

A call to be different

ROY BENJAMIN

Copyright © 2023 Roy Benjamin.

All rights reserved solely by the author. The author guarantees all contents are original and do not infringe upon the legal rights of any other person or work. No part of this book may be reproduced in in any form without the permission of the author.

Unless otherwise indicated, scripture quotations taken from the Holy Bible, New International Version (NIV). © Copyright 1978 by New York International Bible Society.

Used by permission. All rights reserved.

Scripture quotations taken from the King James Version (KJV) – public domain.

ISBN: 979-8-88640-953-6 (sc)
ISBN: 979-8-88640-954-3 (hc)
ISBN: 979-8-88640-955-0 (e)

Because of the dynamic nature of the Internet, any web addresses or links contained in this book may have changed since publication and may no longer be valid. The views expressed in this work are solely those of the author and do not necessarily reflect the views of the publisher, and the publisher hereby disclaims any responsibility for them.

One Galleria Blvd., Suite 1900, Metairie, LA 70001
1-888-421-2397

CONTENTS

Introduction		v
1	**Different People**	1
	Be Different when you give	2
	Be Different when you Pray	3
	Be Different in Forgiving	3
	Be different in Fasting	4
	Be Different in your view of things	5
	Be Focused and Single-minded	5
	Do not Worry	6
	You are Kingdom People	7
2	**Seeing the World Differently**	9
3	**Think Differently**	11
	Transformation Journey	11
	Think and Plan	12
	Mind Matters	13
	Change your Mind	14
4	**Speak Differently**	15
	Express your convictions	15
	Announce your intentions	16
	Testify about your past triumphs	16
	Admit your limitations	17
	Affirm your authority	17
	Declare your victory	18
5	**Love Differently**	19
6	**Lead Differently**	21
7	**Serve Differently**	23

8	**Different Decisions**	27
	Joseph	27
	Esther	28
	Ruth	30
	Shadrach, Meshach, and Abednego	32
	Daniel	33
9	**Different Stories**	35
10	**Different Perspectives**	37
11	**Different Outcomes**	39
12	**Different Responses**	43
13	**Different Reasons**	47
	Reason to Roam	47
	Reason to Repent	48
	Reason to Return	48
	Reason to Celebrate	49
14	**A Different Way**	51
15	**A Different Spirit**	55
16	**Making a Difference**	59
17	**Displaying the Difference**	61
About the Author		63

INTRODUCTION

We are living in a time when most people are trying to blend in and to be like the rest. The thought is that if you look like them and act like them then you will be accepted and loved and become part of the group.

The call for sameness and oneness is especially appealing to those who want to be accepted and are looking for a place to belong.

A person may be criticized or ridiculed for being different. They are questioned why they speak different and act different. The message is that even though it may be difficult being different, it's ok to be different.

By being different, one doesn't have to create dissention or division. You must understand that your thoughts and beliefs will affect your actions and behavior, therefore, you must be willing to stand on the principles and live by them consistently even if you are criticized.

There are times when change is necessary. Change results in making things different to what they were previously. A cook buys food at the grocery store in its natural state. The food then goes through a preparation process where it is washed, seasoned, baked, steamed, or boiled. When it is taken from the stove or oven. It is different to what it was at the store. The things that occurred during the process, and the changes it went through, affects it in a real way and makes it different.

It was raw and plain and dull before the process, now it has a different color, flavor and smell. It was not fit to eat before, but now it is edible. If you tried to eat it before in its former state right off the shelf, you would likely get sick. That food is now distinctively different.

When a person buys a house that is dilapidated, it's usually because they see the potential in it. With some remodeling and refurbishing, the house takes on a new look and is different. The people in the neighborhood who saw it before and knew the condition it was in previously, will comment on how different it looks. The value of the property goes up and it is now appealing and comfortable. It is in a different state and has new purpose.

The same thing happens to a person who comes to faith in Christ. They are converted and transformed. The apostle Paul describes the change that occurs and states that if anyone is in Christ, they are a new creation. The old is gone, the new has come.

That's what it means to be different. People are reborn and renewed and they become different.

As you read this book, you will understand what it means to be different and how the change happens.

Chapter 1

DIFFERENT PEOPLE

God was talking to the prophet Malachi about the people who would experience His blessings and those who would be spared from judgement. He was saying that there was a clear difference between the faithful and believing who put their faith and trust in Him and those who were wicked and not serving God. He stated clearly that they would have different outcomes.

He declared that there would be a day when He would come to intervene in the affairs of men and the people who were living in obedience to His commands and not engaging in evil and wrongdoing, will be rewarded like His treasured possessions, and He will spare them from judgement just as a father has compassion and spares his child who serves him.

He declared that at the time of judgement there will be a clear distinction between the righteous and the wicked, between those who serve God and those who do not.

At the Sermon on the Mount, Jesus was having a session with His disciples. He shared with them the characteristics of His real genuine followers and what they should look like. He indicated that they were people of His kingdom and should act and live like who they were. He talked about the people who were pretenders and actors. He referred to them as hypocrites. Throughout his sermon, He pleaded with His disciples to be different from those people. His admonition to them was that they should not be like them.

He gave some specific guidelines how they should be different from the people who were just putting on a show and doing things for the praise of men and for recognition of their work.

Be Different when you give

The religious leaders and wealthy rulers in Jesus' time were very boastful and arrogant. They displayed their acts of service for everyone to see. As they gave their offerings in the synagogue, they would hold it high and display it so that those present could see what they were giving and how much they were giving. When they gave donations to the needy, they would make a big announcement of their gifts so that people would hear about it and congratulate and honor them for their generosity. Their motives for giving were wrong and they were not sincere in their actions.

Jesus warned His disciples about making a big display of their gifts. He taught them that when they give to the needy, they should not let their left hand know what their right hand was doing and to give their donations privately for God the Father, who sees what is done privately, will reward them publicly.

In this day of television and social media, there is a lot of fundraising and campaigns for various charitable causes. These are good and worthy efforts. However, there are a lot of people who must pose for the camera with their gifts in hand to show that they are giving and make announcements about their offerings. This is good for public relations and advertising but as kingdom people, there must be a difference in giving.

It must be genuine and sincere from a heart of love and compassion. It should be so secretive that while one is giving their offering with the right hand, the left hand is not aware of the contents or the amount that is given. There should not be announcements or advertising of the gifts for publicity or recognition.

When a person gives in secret. God will reward them openly and there must be a difference in the motives and actions of giving.

Be Different when you Pray

The religious leaders did not only make a big show of their giving but when it was time to pray, they ensured that they were seen and heard. Their prayers consisted of loud and babbling lines which they repeated over and again. They elevated their voices so that they could be heard from afar and even created special gurgling sounds to give an impression of super spirituality and special connection to God.

They prayed long prayers because they wanted to be commended for their high-sounding sentences and elaborate prayers.

Jesus exhorted the disciples to be different from the people who kept on repeating and saying the same phrases and cliches.

He told them that when they have their prayer time, they should go to their rooms, close the door, and pray to the Father in private with sincere prayers from their hearts.

On a visit to some prayer meetings in the Christian church, you will hear the same prayers being said each time. People are not praying real prayers. They recite the same prayers that they've been saying for many years. They start yelling as if God is deaf and they change their tone and voice to sound more holy and spiritual. The prayers are centered on personal needs rather than the corporate needs of the church and community. Prayer meetings has become a place where people try to outdo each other and have resorted to rambling words.

It is important to listen to the words of Jesus - do not keep repeating these prayers, for the Father knows what is needed even before the prayer is made.

Be different in praying.

Be Different in Forgiving

As Jesus continued His sermon, He gave the disciples a model prayer that they should pray to God the Father in heaven. A significant part of that prayer is asking God to forgive the debts that is owed to Him and to give us the grace to forgive those who are debtors to us.

This is consistent with the story He told about a servant who owed a large amount of money to his master. He went to the master asking for debt forgiveness. The master forgave his debt, and he was now clear and free.

He later met a colleague who owed him some money and demanded that he pay him instantly. The man pleaded for some time to get the funds together to pay him. He refused to give him time and had him thrown into debtor's prison until he could pay the debt. The master heard about what happened and confronted the man about what he had done to his colleague. He reminded him that he was shown mercy and was forgiven of his debt, but now, he was not willing to extend that same kindness to his colleague.

The Bible encourages us to be forgiving for if you forgive other people when they sin against you, your heavenly Father will also forgive you. But if you do not forgive others their sins, your Father will not forgive your sins.

There are many people who are troubled and depressed because they are carrying around a weight of unforgiveness. They have not released the person who hurt or wronged them previously.

There is power in forgiveness and when we offer forgiveness, then we will receive forgiveness. Forgiveness makes us different people.

Be different in Fasting

There were periods of fasting in the early church. Some of the people that fasted went over and above in their observance of the fast. They would go around looking devout and self-righteous. They poured oil over their heads that would run down their faces so that others would see that they are fasting.

Jesus told his disciples that such rituals and ceremonies were not necessary because this time of fasting was between them and God and that what they were doing was a sacrifice from the heart and not an outward show. He admonished them to wash up, dress up and act normal, for the Father in heaven knows what they were doing, and He will reward them accordingly.

The message is that fasting times are not show times. It is a time of commitment and surrender to the will of God. The key is that God sees the heart and He knows the reason for the fast

Be Different in your view of things

Many of us have seen the TV show where people gather stuff and keep on hoarding it. The more they get, the more they accumulate.

We probably know of people like that in real life who keep storing and adding to their collection. Eventually they get overwhelmed with the amount of stuff, and it becomes a burden.

There are things in life that we treasure and enjoy. It is okay to have things and own stuff. The issue here, is when it takes over our lives and we have so much that it overwhelms us.

Jesus taught His disciples in this lesson that they should not be occupied with storing up treasures on earth, because eventually moths and vermin will infest them and destroy them. He reminded them that thieves could break in and steal that which they have worked hard for and treasure greatly.

They should instead store up treasures in heaven, where insects and bugs cannot destroy them, and where thieves cannot access them.

The thought is, that people get preoccupied with their treasure and their hearts are set on not only hoarding what they already have but they are intensely absorbed in seeking for more.

The advice is that one must be different in their approach to possessions. Hold to that which is lasting and beneficial and let go of that which is worthless and temporal.

Be Focused and Single-minded

One of the biggest problems for humans is to stay focused. The times we live in offer so many options that it is easy to get distracted. There is a need for us to focus on what matters most.

In this culture of multi-tasking, we can drift into areas that waste our time and we do not really accomplish anything significant. The key is to decide what we want to achieve and spend time, effort and sometimes money, on what is beneficial.

Jesus warned His disciples that no one can serve two masters. Either they will hate one and love the other, or they will be devoted to the one and despise the other. He was talking about priorities. The things that we see as important and meaningful.

There comes a time and place where decisions must be made. The choice we make will determine what happens in our future. Some of these can be life changing and affect our lives in a significant way.

He touched on the matter of allegiance when He said that it was impossible for a person to serve two masters. This is a call for total commitment to one and absolute rejection of the other.

The test of the heart is our devotion to one or the other. He gave two examples of masters when He said that a person cannot serve both God and money in the same way.

Because of the world we live in, and the way it is structured, we need money for the daily necessities of life. It allows us to acquire the things we need for ourselves and our families.

Jesus wanted the disciples to understand that when there is a decision about who and what takes precedence in our lives, God must always have the preeminence.

The thing that makes us different people is what is most important to us and where we place our emphasis. We become what we focus on.

Do not Worry

Jesus was a great storyteller and shared a wonderful illustration with the disciples.

He took them to the fields on the mountainside and pointed to a flock of birds feeding in the field. He indicated that they did not have to sow or reap or store up provisions in barns, for the heavenly Father feeds them.

He reminded them that they were much more valuable than the birds and they should not worry about food and clothes, for just as the Father fed and clothed the birds, He will do the same, and much more for them.

He turned around and there was a beautiful patch of flowers growing on the side of the mountain. He looked at them and commented that they did not produce their clothing, but they were dressed in fine garments.

He told them very clearly that God is the one who clothes the grass of the field, which is here today, and tomorrow is thrown into the fire, He will provide clothes, food, shelter, and money.

He concluded the message by saying they should not worry about food, drink or clothes and do not worry about tomorrow, for tomorrow will worry about itself. Each day has enough trouble of its own.

When a person understands this message and lives it out. They will live differently.

You are Kingdom People

The greatest lesson that Jesus taught to His disciples is that even though they were born on this earth and grew up in a certain region, really, they were Kingdom people.

He told them to seek His kingdom first and pursue righteousness, and everything else will fall into place.

He knew that once they understood their heritage and where they belong, they will act differently, think differently, and speak differently because Kingdom people are different.

Kingdom people are Joyful.

Kingdom people are Kind.

Kingdom people are Loving.

Kingdom people are Compassionate.

Kingdom people are Caring.

Kingdom people are Servants.

Chapter 2

SEEING THE WORLD DIFFERENTLY

There is a story in the New Testament about two men who decided to build houses. They got their plans drawn, laid the foundation and started building.

The houses were completed, and they were beautiful. The owners occupied the homes and enjoyed living with their families. Sometime later, the rainy season came along with a windstorm. After the storm passed and the rain ceased, one house was standing firm and secure while the other collapsed.

The house that survived the storm, was built on a rock foundation. The other homeowner wanted a beachfront view, so he built his house on the sand. Both houses looked good and were very spacious and comfortable. The difference in the houses was the foundation on which they were built.

This story indicates the mindset of the two builders. While one was concerned about the view of the ocean, the access to the beach and the praise of friends and family who would come to visit and talk about how lovely the surroundings were and the wonderful scenery overlooking the water.

The other builder was concerned about stability and security of the building. Even though it may have taken a little while longer, he made sure the pillars went down firmly into the rock.

Both of them had beautiful houses but they had a different value system. They looked at the process differently and as a result, there were different outcomes.

There are a lot of lessons that we can learn from this story:

Although we would like to have a beautiful house, having a secure foundation is much more important.

It's not where we build that matters but rather what we're building on.

Life is like the houses. If you build on the rock, it will stand. If you build on the sand, it will collapse.

Know that the storm will come one day and when we plan, we must plan for the storm.

It doesn't matter what others think about us as long we know that we're doing the right thing.

Don't be afraid to build differently. Build something that will last.

Chapter 3
THINK DIFFERENTLY

Transformation Journey

Whenever I hear the word transform, I remember growing up in my hometown in the Caribbean. The standard electric power at that time was 220 volts and the appliances that were used had to be at that voltage.

Occasionally, someone would have a refrigerator or washer shipped from the US territories and those appliances operated on 110 volts. The user would then have to purchase a transformer that would convert the voltage to the required operating standard.

Paul the apostle, in his various writings, talks a lot about transformation. In his letter to the Romans, he advised them not to copy the behavior and customs of this world, but let God transform them into a new person by changing their way of thinking. He appealed to them to behave differently, and this behavioral change would happen by a new way of thinking. In another translation it is described as the renewing of the mind.

Transformation happens when a person thinks differently. He continued in this trend as he gave them another challenging insight that they should not think that they are better than they really are but do an honest evaluation of themselves.

Paul not only writes about thinking differently to the Romans, but he gives the same message to the Philippians. He pleaded with them to fix their thoughts on things that are true, honorable, right, pure, and admirable. Things that are excellent and commendable should be on their minds. He also appealed to them not to be selfish or try to impress others but be humble and think about others.

He called for them to have the same attitude that Christ Jesus had, taking an interest in others, and not just thinking about themselves.

He understood that when people developed the same mindset as Jesus, there would be a difference in how they see themselves and see others. It is all about attitude and approach.

Another important aspect of the transformation journey is what I call the focus factor.

You become what you focus on. What you think about, speak about, and concentrate on will eventually shape the way you live.

If you want to live differently, you must think differently.

Think and Plan

One day while Jesus was teaching, a man in the crowd shouted out to Him that He should speak to his brother about dividing the family inheritance in an equitable manner. Jesus responded that He was not going to judge the matter.

He warned the man to be careful about how he thought about material things, and he should guard his heart against greed and covetousness because real living is not about the things that one owns or accomplishes.

To emphasize this concept, Jesus told them a story about a rich farmer who had an abundant harvest. This large crop brought about a storage problem for the farmer, as his current barn did not have sufficient space to store the crop.

He came up with a plan to expand his storage facility that would allow him to store his harvest and provide capacity for future crops.

This would bring large profits and allow him to go into retirement and enjoy the rest of his years in ease and comfort.

The plan sounded good because the farmer had worked hard and put a lot of time and money into his business. It seemed like the perfect situation, and this would bring the peace and happiness that he had been thinking about.

Jesus called this plan foolish thinking. He said that life is not just about wealth, possessions, and net worth. He commented that the man had not factored in the possibility of dying and the riches that he had accumulated would pass to someone else.

The point of Jesus' story was that if a person only thinks about money, wealth and business and does not include God as an integral part of his life, it is all in vain and is not worth the time and effort.

His point is that while we must think about the things of life and plan. We should also include God in our plans and live with eternity on our minds.

Mind Matters

Many people are very aware and conscious of what they feed into their bodies. Those who suffer from various illnesses are concerned about diet restrictions and the type of food they consume,

Others are concerned about their weight and avoid foods that will add to their body fat.

In the same manner, we must be careful about what we feed our minds. The time spent watching TV, being on social media or even online games can contribute greatly to our levels of anxiety and stress.

We have heard the statement that whatever goes into our minds, will eventually come out in our actions. If we want to grow and develop, we must focus on the things that will contribute to our wellbeing.

Our thought life is very important, and we must give serious attention to exercise the mind and allow it to grow and expand.

Change your Mind

Change does not come easy because we have a belief system that was instilled in us from childhood. The things that we see and hear as well as that which we have been doing for decades is now so deeply embedded, that it is difficult to think outside of that which we've become accustomed to.

It is not easy to shift from what we know and understand to that which is unfamiliar and different. We avoid paths that are strange, and only stick to that which is easy and comfortable.

There are times we are called to go into unknown territory, and this creates anxiety and discomfort because it requires rethinking and relearning, and that can be difficult.

The key to making the adjustment in moving forward and upward is to be willing to think differently and change our minds.

It requires determination and discipline to develop a pattern of excellence and live the way you were created to be. It is doable and worth the effort.

Chapter 4

SPEAK DIFFERENTLY

Everyone loves the story of David and Goliath because they enjoy the idea of the underdog beating the champion. It is a story of the least likely overcoming the obvious favorite.

No one could see David beating Goliath, and certainly, not killing him.

David knew he had the victory and was not afraid to speak about it.

Express your convictions

The Philistines and the Israelites were at war, and David's brothers had gone to battle. David was the youngest brother and not eligible for military duty, so he stayed at home to take care of the family's farm.

His father sent him on a mission to take supplies for his brothers and to bring back a report of how they were doing. While he was at the battlefield delivering the supplies for his brothers, Goliath who was a giant and champion of the Philistines came out from their camp and started boasting and taunting the Israelites.

The soldiers ran in fear of the man and complained about his intimidating tactics. When David saw this, he went to the men and inquired who the giant was and what reward would be given for the person who kills him and end this ongoing standoff.

His oldest brother heard him questioning the soldiers and engaging in a discussion about the Philistine warrior and details of the battle. He was very angry and told David that since he did not understand military affairs, he had no business in this discussion with trained soldiers. He was just a shepherd boy, and this was out of his league.

David stood up and spoke to his brother that this was a challenge to Israel, therefore it was a challenge to him, and he had a right to speak up. He was convinced that this was a cause to speak about and he was going to speak about his convictions.

There are times at the risk of ridicule and negative comments, we must speak about the things that affect us and make a statement for truth and justice.

Announce your intentions

The soldiers overheard what David said and reported it to Saul, who sent for David to hear what he had to say.

David spoke to Saul and told him that he was going to fight Goliath and that no one should be afraid or lose heart because of the giant.

Saul looked at David and replied that he was just a young boy and the giant had been a warrior since his youth and never lost a battle.

He stated that David was no match for Goliath and would not be able to go up against him. This did not deter David because he knew that he could win the battle and he was not afraid to speak up.

Testify about your past triumphs

At this point David decided to let Saul know about his past experiences. Even though he was not a trained soldier or qualified for service, he had the heart of a warrior.

He told him about his job on the farm keeping his father's sheep. He shared about the time when a lion attacked the flock and carried off a sheep. He pursued the lion, struck it down and rescued the sheep from its mouth. He went on to describe how the lion turned on him and he seized it by its hair and killed it.

He looked Saul in the eye and declared that just as he had killed the lion who came after his sheep, he will kill Goliath who is challenging the army of Israel.

Saul was impressed with his story, gave him his blessing, and sent him to fight Goliath.

Admit your limitations

One of the things that distinguishes a soldier who goes to war, is their uniform. When a soldier signs up for duty, they are given the uniform and all the gear that goes along with it.

That's exactly what happened here. Once David committed to the fight, he was given the Israelite army uniform along with a helmet and sword.

He put on the uniform, attached the sword, and tried walking around. The uniform did not fit because it was too large, the helmet was uncomfortable, and he could not walk with the sword.

He tried marching around a few more times and then looked at the commanding officer and told him he could not go to fight in that uniform because it did not fit and he was not comfortable in it. He took off the military uniform and put back on his shepherd's coat, got his staff in his hand and went down to the river, chose five smooth stones, and put them in his bag along with his sling.

David knew that the uniform would not work for him, and he was not ashamed or afraid to admit it and go for what he had tried and proven in his previous battle.

Speak about your limitations and let go of the thing that is holding you back from living your best life. Use what you have and fight with all your strength.

Affirm your authority

The soldiers had run away from the giant and there was no one who wanted to fight with him. That day Goliath came out as usual, David marched out to the battlefield. The Philistine looked at him scornfully and felt insulted that a young boy would come up against him.

At a closer look, he did not have any weapon. He only had the stones he gathered at the river and a shepherd's staff.

Goliath yelled out that he would tear him to pieces and give his flesh to the birds for food. On hearing that, a normal person would be scared and retreat.

David kept coming and shouted back at Goliath that although he was equipped with a sword, spear, and javelin, he was coming against him in the name of the Lord Almighty, the God of the armies of Israel.

He declared to the giant and all Israel that he was going to fight this battle with the authority of the Lord God Almighty who is great and powerful.

Declare your victory

Not only did David affirm his authority but he declared that even before the fight started, he'd already won.

He shouted loud for all to hear that the Lord was going to deliver the giant into his hands. He told him that he would strike him down and cut off his head. He announced that he would give the carcasses of the Philistine army to the birds and the wild animals, and the whole world will know that there is a God in Israel.

He declared to all those who were gathered at the battlefield that they will know that it is not only by sword or spear that the Lord saves, but the battle belongs to God and He would give all of them into the hands of the Israelites.

That was a clear declaration of victory.

What are you saying about the battle you're facing right now? Have you surrendered to the enemy? Have you given up or you are declaring victory in Jesus' name?

Chapter 5

LOVE DIFFERENTLY

Love is a word that is used frequently. People talk about love, but they are not sure what love is. There are songs about love, but they don't give the meaning of love.

Paul devoted an entire chapter in his letter to the Corinthians to describe love.

When we think of love, we think of feelings, emotions, and moods. Paul defines love as something we do rather than something we feel. Love is action. It does something and makes things happen,

He begins by saying that love is patient. It can withstand malice, criticism, and wrong with no thoughts of anger or bitterness and does not seek revenge,

Love gives one the ability to be longsuffering even when being treated cruelly and unjustly. It allows a person to overcome feelings of anger and animosity and makes them kind to those who offend them.

Love is not boastful and arrogant and does not seek to become proud and haughty or seek to put down others and engage in self-promotion.

Love is considerate and thoughtful. It is respectful of other people's need, and seeks to build up and strengthen, rather than tear down and destroy.

Love gives honor to people and treats them with dignity and respect. It does not hate or discriminate. It is not selective in who gets to benefit.

Love does not stir strife and dissension. Love does not speak with angry words and foul language to another person.

Love does not rejoice in wrongdoing and is not preferential or partial in its judgement of others.

Love is decent and behaves in a reverent and respectful manner to all people.

Love avoids environments of chaos and confusion and seeks for order and discipline. It is always for peace.

Love is not rude and does not treat people with disdain and scorn. Love is considerate of other people's feelings.

Love is not selfish and will not trample on others for profit or pleasure. Love gives and seeks for the wellbeing and happiness of others.

Love does not use the privilege and position of one's office to crush other people's hopes, dreams, and aspirations. Love encourages, promotes, and inspire others to greatness.

Love does not rejoice over the failures and shortcomings of others, but it covers over their weakness and mistakes and help them to become better people.

Love is thrilled to see people doing well and celebrates their achievements.

If someone was blessed with all the spiritual gifts and could speak in tongues and do miracles. It still would not count for anything because love supersedes all the gifts.

The gift of tongues, prophecy and knowledge will cease but love never ends.

Love is the greatest gift one can have. Love makes a difference.

Chapter 6

LEAD DIFFERENTLY

There are many people who were born with a natural gift of leadership. Others develop leadership over time and through different circumstances. Some leaders take on the responsibility because they are thrust into the role and step up to do the job.

There are people in leadership positions who are not leaders. They take on the job because it looks glamorous, and they enjoy the spotlight.

Being a leader requires not only ability and skill but approach and aptitude.

Leaders must be fearless. The path is not always clear and because one does not have an understanding where they are and where they are going. It is difficult to lead others to a place that you are not familiar.

It is a risk to go to a place that is unchartered territory, and there is no direction or map to guide you. You will have to make a path and then give direction to people to follow you along that road. There may be mistakes and you may lose your way at times, but great leaders are not afraid to admit their mistakes or turn around and find a way to get through.

Leadership is lonely. Most times you are all by yourself and there is no one to share with, talk to, or consult with. These are the times that you learn to go deep inside and keep moving forward even if no one else is there.

Leaders are people of integrity. Because it looks good doesn't mean it's good for you, Leaders are held to high standards because people follow what they do. The leader should always do the right thing no matter the cost.

Leaders stands up for their people. The people you lead, look to you for guidance and direction. They will fail sometimes and not come through when you need them, but these are opportunities to bring them along and help them grow and develop.

There's a difference between leaders and bosses. Leaders help people to improve and become better at what they do. Bosses are there to ensure people do their jobs and complete their tasks.

A leader is a servant. They serve the people they lead and serve the people they work for. They have a servant's heart and are always ready to assist, support and enable people to do their jobs well.

A leader is a professional. They do not get petty and personal. They do not pick unnecessary fights and they are not loud, rowdy, and obnoxious.

A leader is a visionary. They look way ahead and see things no one else sees and encourages their people to go forward and get to that place.

Leaders care deeply. They care about their job; they care about the people they lead and they care about the people they work for. They care about their families.

Leaders are people of action. They don't just talk about it, but they get things done and make it happen.

Leaders are for change and transformation. They are constantly making old things new.

There is a difference between a manager and a distinctive leader. They make a difference.

Chapter 7

SERVE DIFFERENTLY

There was a well-travelled road between Jerusalem and Jericho. People transported goods along the road, and they would go back and forth to take care of their business.

It was also a dangerous road, as bandits hid along the way waiting for an occasion to rob those who were travelling along the road.

This good gentleman was going down that road and a gang of thieves attacked him, robbed him, beat him, and left him half dead on the side of the road.

They stripped him of his clothes, so he was also naked and exposed to the elements. He was in a very bad condition.

The road was not only travelled by businessmen and robbers, but religious leaders also went back and forth to carry out their duties at the temple.

A priest happened to be going along the road and saw the man lying on the side, bleeding, and moaning. He was on his way to officiate at the meeting of the synagogue. He had his ceremonial duties to perform, and he concluded that he could not defile himself with this bleeding wounded man. He was thinking about being on time for the service and getting his congregation together.

This was a great opportunity to serve a dying man and help him in his time of crisis. However, his job at the temple was more important, and assisting someone who was hurt was not a priority.

A Levite came down the road also and heard the wounded man cry out. He went over to where he was lying but instead of reaching out and helping, he hurried off. He was probably concerned that the robbers might return, and he could become the next victim.

Both men held positions of sacred office and part of their duties were to serve people and help them in the situations of life . This time, they both failed in carrying out the responsibilities of their calling and walked away from an opportunity to open their hearts, show mercy, and extend help to someone who needed it most.

A Samaritan came along the same road. He was from a place that the Jews hated and despised. The Jews had no relations with the Samaritans, but this man wasn't concerned about nationality or ethnicity.

He saw the condition of the man and his heart was filled with compassion and he went over to him.

This Samaritan, like the priest and Levite, saw the man in a state of helplessness but unlike them, he had compassion on him and went over to where he was, cleaned up his bleeding wounds. He took oil and poured it in to help stop the bleeding. He applied some of the wine he was carrying which would serve as an antiseptic.

He wrapped up the wounds to prevent it from infection and put the man on his donkey.

I'm certain the Samaritan was not carrying an emergency kit with medical supplies to treat the man. He had to come up with makeshift stuff to attend to the victim. Since he did not have bandages or cleaning wipes, he must have torn some strips from his garment to use.

The oil and wine he poured on the wound were products he was either taking to market to sell or these were goods he had purchased and was on his way home.

These products were costly, and it was a sacrifice for him to use them on a stranger.

He put the man on his donkey. Since the man was wounded and really in bad shape, He had to be lifted on to the donkey. This took a lot of effort.

Both men were not able ride on the donkey. The Samaritan walked so that the man could be transported by the donkey.

He realized the man needed rest and sleep after the traumatic experience he had been through. He took him to an inn where he could get some food and rest and have a time to heal.

He gave the inn keeper two denarii which is the equivalent of two days wages, to cover expenses for the time he would be at the inn. He also promised to reimburse him for any extra expense above that which he had already given him.

Consider the likelihood that the Samaritan never met the wounded man before and had no obligation to do anything to help him, yet he went over and above and gave his best.

The priest and Levite declined to show compassion, although they must have studied the prophets and read the writings of Micah where he stated:

"With what shall I come before the Lord, and bow myself before God on high? Shall I come before him with burnt offerings, with calves a year old? Will the Lord be pleased with thousands of rams, with ten thousand of rivers of oil Shall I give my firstborn for my transgression, the fruit of my body for the sin of my soul?" He has told you, O man, what is good; and what does the Lord require of you but to do justice, and to love kindness, and to walk humbly with your God?"

This is the true spirit of service, when you give your best to those who deserve it the least for as you're serving others, you are serving Christ the Lord who will reward you for your service.

The truth is, we do not serve for rewards, we serve because we are distinctly different.

Chapter 8
DIFFERENT DECISIONS

Joseph

Joseph was sold by his brothers to Ishmaelite traders who took him to Egypt and sold him as a slave. He ended up in the house of Potiphar, the head of Pharaoh's security guards,

He applied himself and worked diligently at the tasks that were given to him and Potiphar took notice of his ability, work ethics and attitude. He put him in charge of his household and entrusted everything he owned to Joseph's care.

Joseph became a successful man and managed Potiphar's household and his property very well.

Potiphar was impressed with Joseph's work skills, and abilities but his wife admired Joseph's handsome face and well-built body. She approached him with casual compliments and subtle flirts while Joseph remained calm and conducted himself in a professional manner.

The approach by Potiphar's wife changed from being occasional and passing, to become more direct and intentional. She let him know that it was her desire for them to have an intimate affair and became more aggressive in her advances. However, Joseph became firmer in his refusal.

What caused Joseph to make that decision to stand strong and not give in to her wishes? I believe there were four reasons for his decision.

Courage – In the face of what could have been an interesting adventure, he understood the consequences and was willing to stand up for moral integrity. He decided that even though this was an offer that was appealing and enticing, there was too much at risk and he had the courage to say no.

Clear – The other reason Joseph made the decision to say no is that he was very clear about his boundaries. He recognized the fact that even though he oversaw the affairs of the house, she was the wife of his master and there was a line that he would not cross.

Conviction – He had a deep sense of conviction about what he was facing. He called it a great wickedness and a sin against God.

Once he saw it in this way, he knew it was wrong and he refused to do it.

Commitment – It's one thing to talk about it but it's another thing to be about it. Potiphar's wife got to the point that she wasn't just suggesting anymore that they go to bed and have an illicit sexual relationship. She was serious about it and one day she grabbed him and told him that she was tired of begging, and she was commanding him to submit to her wishes. She grabbed him by the cloak he was wearing, and he left his garment in her hand and ran from the house.

She accused him of rape, and he ended up serving time in prison. Sometimes the decision you make will cost you.

Joseph decided that he was going to hold on to his dignity and integrity and let the garment go. He was committed to purity, and he made a different decision.

Esther

The story of Esther is very intriguing. It tells about a Persian king who became very unhappy with his wife because she refused to obey his orders. He decided to replace her with another queen that would be more compliant. He organized a beauty contest and brought the most beautiful women of the kingdom from which he would select his new queen.

Esther was chosen as one of the women that would go through the selection process. She was a Jew and the adopted daughter of Mordecai who was brought to Persia as a captive prisoner during the war.

At the end of the of the beauty contest, Esther won the favor and approval of the king, and he made her his queen. This was a big win for Mordecai and Esther.

She had not revealed her nationality and background because Mordecai had forbidden her to do so.

There was a man in the Persian kingdom who received a huge promotion and was given a seat of honor higher than any other official. He was held in very high esteem and all the royal officials at the king's gate would kneel and pay him honor. Mordecai refused to honor him, and Haman was very annoyed.

Haman discovered that Mordecai was a Jew and he looked for an opportunity to get back at him. He decided to not only kill Mordecai but destroy all the Jews who were Mordecai's people.

Haman went to the king and reported that the Jews were not being loyal, they had different customs and they could become a threat which the king should address by killing them and this would eliminate any threat.

The king signed an order to destroy, kill and exterminate the Jews .

Mordecai heard about the order and was deeply distressed. He sent a message to Esther that she should go to the king and intercede on behalf of the Jewish people.

She sent back to Mordecai that it was not appropriate to just go into the king's court and make that kind of request. One must be summoned into his presence and the king must extend his golden rod as a sign of his approval.

She also reported that she had not been called into the king's presence for thirty days.

When the word got back to Mordecai, he replied that even though she was the queen and living in the king's palace, this did not make her immune from the king's order because she was a Jew and subject to elimination like the other Jews.

He encouraged her not to remain silent and reminded her that she was placed in that position and was in the palace for that particular purpose as an intercessor and mediator.

When Esther received the challenge from Mordecai, she requested a time of prayer and fasting on her behalf and she and her servants would also fast as she considered this a very serious assignment.

She then made a declaration that she would take the matter to the king even if it meant risking her life. She came to a point where she realized that this was a critical moment that required her to make a different decision.

Ruth

I am always fascinated by stories that begin with tragedy, loss, and impossible situations, and as it continues, it takes a turn and evolves into something filled with hope, triumph, and positive outcomes.

If you ever read the book of Ruth, you will see this pattern played out through the chapters. The very first verse begins with a famine in the land. Although most of us have been through times where certain food items were scarce or unavailable for a period. I don't believe many of us have lived through a famine.

This food shortage was so severe that Elimelech decided to move his family to another country to survive the famine. The place they moved to was not friendly territory. This was considered a heathen place, but some people would reason that a man has got to do something to keep his family alive. It was a tough reality.

I believe that Elimelech was an ambitious man and a hard worker. He was there to provide for his family, and he put every effort into it. In the process, he died and Naomi, his wife was left with her two sons.

The boys grew up and married two women from Moab, the place where they relocated. They lived in Moab for about ten years and then both sons also died, and Naomi was left alone.

DIFFERENT DECISIONS

As time went by, she got news that things were beginning to turn around in Bethlehem where she was originally from. The famine had ceased, and the food crops were growing again.

She planned to return home and Orpah and Ruth, offered to travel back with her. They set off on their journey and was travelling for some time when Naomi had a talk with them. They talked about their deceased husbands and reminisced about the times they had together, and she thanked them for the time they had shared and their kindness to her and the family. She then encouraged them to return to Moab to be with their families.

She wished them all the best and prayed that they would get new husbands because she was not going to marry again and have more sons that they could marry. She advised that they should return and restart their lives. They hugged and cried in each other's arms, and they insisted that they would go with her back to her country.

They wept aloud again then Orpah kissed Naomi goodbye and returned. Ruth embraced Naomi and held on to her. Naomi pleaded with her to follow Orpah and return to her home. Ruth replied that she was not going back and would not leave her because she had decided to follow her wherever she went, she would live with her wherever she lived and that she would be part of her people. She further declared that she would accept and worship her God and would die and be buried in the same place as her and she made a vow to stay with her for life.

They both continued together and got to Bethlehem. The people remembered Naomi and greeted her. She responded that she had been through so much hurt and bitterness, that she preferred to be called Mara instead of Naomi.

They arrived in Bethlehem as the barley harvest was beginning, Naomi had a relative whose name was Boaz and he owned one of the largest fields.

Naomi encouraged Ruth to go to work in the field of Boaz and help to gather the harvest. When Boaz went to the field to greet the harvesters, he inquired about Ruth and was told that she was related to Naomi and had returned with her from Moab.

Boaz went to directly to her, welcomed her and invited her to stay in his field and partake of the benefits of the farm. He made sure that she had enough for her and Naomi to eat. He provided protection for her and proper work conditions in the field.

The story continues where Boaz marries Ruth, and they have a son together. Ruth was the great grandmother of David who became king of Israel.

When you make a decision that is different, it leads to an outcome that is also different.

Shadrach, Meshach, and Abednego

King Nebuchadnezzar made an image of gold, ninety feet high and nine feet wide and erected it in Babylon. He announced that all the officials were to attend the unveiling ceremony.

He sent out a proclamation that at the sound of the music, everyone must bow down and worship the image and whoever does not bow down, and worship will immediately be thrown into a blazing furnace.

On the day of the dedication of the image, the people bowed down and worshipped it.

There were some Jews who had been brought to Babylon and placed in official positions. While the ceremony was taking place and the other officials were participating and bowing down, these Jews refused to bow down or worship the image.

The others who noticed what was happening, went to the king and complained that the Jewish officials were not bowing down. They reminded him that the punishment for non-compliance was to be thrown into the fiery furnace.

The king summoned the Jewish officials, whose names were Shadrach, Meshach and Abednego and he enquired whether the report he had received was true.

They replied that the report was true and that they were not going to bow down to the image. The king was furious at this act of defiance and told them he would give them another chance to obey.

They repeated to King Nebuchadnezzar that they did not need to defend themselves in this matter. They told him that if they were thrown into the blazing furnace, the God whom they served was able to deliver them from it, and that He would deliver them. However, if he does not deliver them, they still would not worship the image of gold that he had set up.

The king ordered the furnace heated seven times hotter than usual and had the men bound and thrown in the into the blazing furnace.

God showed up in the furnace with the men, delivered them from the heat of the fire and Nebuchadnezzar ordered them to be freed from the furnace.

Making different decisions is hard and has harsh consequences but, in the end, there will be victory.

Daniel

King Darius appointed several governors to rule throughout his kingdom. He also selected three senior officials to whom these governors would report to, and Daniel was appointed as one those officials. He stood out from the other officials, and he was distinguished above them because he had a good attitude and an excellent spirit.

The king recognized his approach and planned to set him over the whole kingdom. The high officials and the governors were not happy with the king's decision and sought to find a ground for complaint against Daniel regarding the kingdom, but they could find no ground for complaint or any fault, because he was faithful, and a man of integrity.

These men concluded that they could not find any ground for complaint against Daniel regarding his work. However, they figured out that they could find something about his religious beliefs and practices since he was a believer and prayed consistently.

The high officials discussed this matter and agreed that they would approach the king and get him to sign a law that would conflict with Daniel's prayer life. They told the king that he should establish a decree and enforce an injunction, that whoever makes petition to any god or man for thirty days, except to the king, will be thrown into the den of lions. They petitioned him that he should issue the decree and put it in writing so that it cannot be altered, according to the law of the Medes and the Persians, which cannot be revoked. King Darius signed the document and ordered it into law.

Daniel learned that the document had been signed and published. He went home to his upstairs room where the windows opened toward Jerusalem. Three times a day he got down on his knees and prayed, giving thanks to his God, just as he had done previously.

The men conspired together, went to Daniel's house, and found him praying to his God. They approach the king, concerning the order he had signed and reported that Daniel was in violation of the law and continued praying three times daily. They reminded him that that this was the law of the Medes and Persians and that no ordinance that the king established could be changed.

The king gave the order to throw Daniel in the lion's den and sealed the door.

The king was concerned about Daniel's fate and did not sleep well that night. Very early the next morning, he went to the lion's den and shouted out to Daniel enquiring whether he was still alive. Daniel responded that the God to whom he was praying continually, had sent His angels, and delivered him from the lions.

The king commanded them to free Daniel from the lions' den. He came out without being hurt or scratched.

He made a different decision and it cost him a night in the lion's den, but it proved to the king and his accusers that being different doesn't mean that you will be destroyed,

Chapter 9

DIFFERENT STORIES

We often repeat the phrase that is included in the Declaration of Independence that all men are created equal. While we recognize and affirm this, we are also aware that there are different situations which people find themselves in and this contributes to different stories in their lives.

The Israelites had grown to be a large population in Egypt and the Egyptian leaders were fearful of their numbers and the possibility of an uprising. He was concerned that they would conspire with his enemies and fight against them. To mitigate the perceived threat, they put slave masters over the Israelites to oppress them with forced labor.

The Israelites groaned in their slavery and cried out to God, who heard their prayer and raised up Moses to help deliver them and bring them out of Egypt.

When Moses approached Pharaoh to free the people and allow them to leave Egypt, Pharaoh hardened his heart and would not let them go.

This resulted in God sending a series of plagues on the land of Egypt to get the attention of the Egyptians. As the plagues were taking over the land, God made some specific arrangements for the Israelites.

He allowed swarms of flies to descend on Egypt, but he told Moses on that day when the flies came, He will deal differently with Goshen, where the Israelites lived. There were no swarms of flies there. God made a distinction between the Egyptians and the Israelites.

When the plague came upon the livestock, all the livestock of the Egyptians died, but not one animal belonging to the Israelites died.

Throughout Egypt, hail struck everything in the fields—both people and animals; it beat down everything growing in the fields and stripped every tree. The only place where there was no hail was Goshen.

When the final and most significant plague was about to come upon Egypt, God gave specific instructions to the Israelites. He told them that they should put a mark of blood over the doorframes of their houses which would be a sign for the death angel who would sweep over the land. When he goes through to strike down the Egyptians, he will see the blood on the top and sides of the doorframe and will pass over that house. He would not permit the destroyer to enter the houses and strike the firstborn of the Israelites.

Every firstborn son in Egypt died, from the firstborn son of Pharaoh, who was the king, to the firstborn son of the ordinary people, and all the firstborn of the cattle as well. There was a loud cry throughout Egypt but there was not any loss of life in the Israelite territory.

God delivered the Israelite from of the plagues and Pharaoh eventually changed his mind and allowed the Israelites to leave Egypt and be free from bondage.

There was a distinctive difference between Egypt and Israel.

Chapter 10

DIFFERENT PERSPECTIVES

Throughout our lives, we have been trained to look at things in different ways. We are influenced by the things we hear and see. We behave and act according to our belief system. However, many people remain fixed in a particular custom or lifestyle as they're concerned about being different from the rest.

The major institutions in our society play a major role in shaping and inspiring some of these perceptions. Their messages and language persuade their followers to go down certain paths and not even question whether it is right or wrong or good or bad.

As part of a church congregation, I am grateful for the opportunity to gather with others for worship and fellowship. However, in the 21st century church, there is a need for a shift and movement so that we can get back to the real purpose we were called to.

Move from an inward focus where the emphasis is on programs, meetings, buildings, and to some extent, money. There should be an outward focus on the community that is declining, our culture that needs attention and our nation that is divided.

Move from being alienated and separated from the communities where we live, to being engaged in the life of the community. There is a need for serving the helpless people and caring for the poor and needy.

Move from "a church against the world" to a "church for the world" where we see ourselves as blessed to be a blessing.

Move from a fearful, pessimistic view of the future to a hopeful, optimistic view of a new heaven and a new earth.

Move from competition with other churches and denominations to kingdom cooperation where we are marching together like a mighty army.

Move from a "one-man-show" leadership style to a priesthood of believers with the emphasis being about servant leadership rather than a "top down" hierarchical style of leadership.

Move from biblical illiteracy to biblical literacy where believers are encouraged to read and study the Bible for themselves rather than quoting texts and phrases from the internet.

Move from focusing on problems to a vision-oriented focus.

Move to ensure that each member identifies one person who they are involved with on a regular basis in discipling and personal development.

Move to increase the church's influence on the non-churched community and encourage new people to be discipled into the fellowship of believers.

Move from using only professionals, to encouraging the proper management and utilization of the gifts and talents among us to have a spirit-led worship experience.

Move from an emphasis on numbers to an emphasis on impacting people, communities, and cultures.

Move from the great commission being understood as saving souls to the great commission being understood as discipling nations.

Move from seeing the church as a place of meeting to seeing it as people called by God who gather for fellowship.

Chapter 11

DIFFERENT OUTCOMES

There is a story in the book of Genesis which gives an insight into the history of mankind. As the human population increased on the earth, they became corrupt and wicked and there was violence in land.

The earth was also filled with cruelty and injustice and there was no rule of law. Everyone had gone in their own way and the evil spread throughout the world.

Man was created as innocent beings, but now immorality and depravity had taken root.

There seemed to be no limit to the corruption and there was no fear of God. The world had plunged into absolute chaos and confusion.

The lawlessness and wickedness did not go unnoticed. Man was living as though they were in control of their affairs but the Almighty God who is Lord of the earth was watching.

There was no fear of God and the people kept going deeper in their evil ways. They were comfortable in their sinful condition.

God was looking on and he was very angry with the condition of man. He was dissatisfied with their lifestyle and behavior.

He was grieved because He had placed mankind here on earth for His glory, but they had become vile and detestable. He decided to destroy all mankind.

During this rebellion and disobedience, there was one person who stood out from the rest. His name was Noah.

He was upright, honest, and a man of integrity. While everyone else was going in their corrupt way and living in contempt of God's laws, Noah was living as a righteous man.

God favored Noah because of his honorable stance, and He was pleased with his life.

He decided to save Noah and his family from the destruction that He was going to bring to the earth. He told him about the impending judgement and gave him an escape plan.

He revealed to Noah that He was going to send a flood on the earth, and everything will be destroyed. He also gave him instructions to build an ark for refuge so that he and his family can live through the flood and come out safe and secure.

Noah had never seen a flood and he was no builder. It was easy for him to question God about the details of the flood and use an excuse that he had no building skills and would not be able to do what He was asking him to do.

The text tells us that Noah did everything that God commanded him to do.

God gave him the blueprint and layout of the ark. He gave specific measurements and design for the building. It took him a while to build the ark, but he completed it.

As God promised, the flood came and destroyed the people of the earth but Noah and his family and all the animals that were in the ark, survived the flood.

I am very sure that Noah had a difficult time living in the place he did. He lived differently to the people around him. Not only was his lifestyle different, but he preached regularly to the people and challenged them about their way of life.

That did not sit well with them, and he was mocked and ridiculed for his way of living and his message.

One day he came out with a different style of preaching. In addition to his regular rebuke about ungodly living, he was now saying that a flood was coming and the whole world would be destroyed.

To make it even worse, he started building an ark in his backyard and invited the people to come in as a shelter from the flood. He became the talk of the town. As the large structure of the ark came into view and the people saw it, they laughed at him and told him he was out of his mind.

The ark was completed, and Noah gathered his family and two of every animal and bird into the ark. When the door was closed, the rain began to fall and the water on the ground rose.

The flood that God promised would come was now present and all those who were not in the ark perished. Noah and his family were safe and alive in the ark.

When you live differently, there will be different outcomes. The message is that there is a distinctive difference between those who live wickedly and those who live uprightly.

Chapter 12
DIFFERENT RESPONSES

There are many different challenges that we will face in life. How we respond to them will determine what happens to us.

We do have a choice in our response to crisis or disaster. It can be fear or faith.

It can be courage or cowering. We decide to stand in the face of difficult situations, or we can run away.

Sometimes the path to the response is not clear and we have to think through the consequences of our decision. There are other times when the stakes are high, and we do not have the time or opportunity to waver.

It is those situations that bring out the best in us and help us understand who we are and what we're made of.

There was a time when the Israelites were in bondage in Egypt and Pharaoh gave a command to kill all the males that were born to them.

This ruling was made because of Pharaoh's fear of the growing population of the Israelites and what could happen if they grew and became strong.

During the time that this order to kill the babies were in effect, a couple from the tribe of Levite gave birth to a son.

When the child was born, there was something about him that got their attention. They saw that he was exceptional and had a different spirit.

Even though he was just a baby, they could tell that he was special. They recognized greatness in him. This child had the mark of a leader and there was a call on his life.

They were also very aware of the ruling to have him killed. However, they were not afraid of the king's command. They knew it would be a risk to disobey the order because if the baby was discovered, they would be killed also.

They decided that the child was worth saving and they would do whatever it took to shield and protect him. They hid him in the house for three months.

At the end of the three-month period, they made a special basket and sealed it to make it waterproof. They put the baby in the basket and took him down to the river and hid him among the tall water shrubs.

They sent his older sister to watch over him and take care of him. This was a big risk, and they were putting everything on the line.

The chances of survival of this baby were slim to none. If they kept him at home, he could be discovered and killed. If they put him in the river, he could drown, or a creature could come and hurt him.

While they must have thought about these possibilities, they had no idea of what would happen next.

The daughter of Pharaoh came down to that same river where the baby was, to bathe. She came to the place where the basket with the baby was floating and sent one of her servants to get it and opened it.

The baby started crying and she felt compassion for him. They observed that it was a Hebrew baby.

The big sister was vigilant and ran to the scene and suggested that she could find someone who could nurse and take care of the baby. Pharaoh's daughter consented and the girl brought the mother of the baby to take care of him.

The princess decided to adopt the baby and gave him the name Moses because he was drawn from the water. Moses grew up in the palace and was officially the prince of Egypt.

Moses' mother was paid to take care of him, but during the time of raising him and nurturing him, she taught him about his heritage and instilled in him the Hebrew values.

These lessons stuck and when he came to the age of maturity, he refused to be a prince of Egypt and sided with the people of Israel. He eventually had to flee Egypt.

He returned later as a leader to deliver the Israelites from Egypt. He led them through the Red Sea and the desert and brought them to the edge of the Promised Land.

The response of Moses' parents to the king's law was the catalyst for all that was to happen later in the history of the Israelites. They decided to defy him and protect their child.

Chapter 13

DIFFERENT REASONS

Reason to Roam

There was a successful businessman who had two sons. They were involved with him in the family business and doing well.

One day the younger son told his dad that he would like to have a meeting with him to talk about his future. During the meeting the son requested the share of money and property that he would inherit as part of the will.

He decided he did not want to wait for his dad to die and receive the inheritance then, He asked his father to do an assessment and give him the portion that would be allotted to him.

The father complied and gave him his portion. The son announced shortly after, that he was going to take a leave of absence and do some travelling.

He packed his belongings and went off on a journey. He decided to have a good time while he had money and opportunity. He invested in a lavish property, bought some of the finest suits, had a nice ride and partied with the best and finest in the city where he moved to.

He made a lot of friends, and he was the talk of the town. Everyone wanted to get to know him. He kept spending and partying. He realized that the funds were getting low, but he kept on splurging.

Reason to Repent

Eventually he was out of money because he spent it all. About the same time there was a famine in the land, and everything was scarce.

The young man was in great need because all his money was gone. He tried to borrow money from his friends and get some assistance from the people he used to hang with, but no one would help him.

Eventually after selling his condo and car and pawning his suits and jewelry, he decided to get a job to keep him from starving. The only job available was at a pig farm and he decided to accept it to keep from starving.

Things were so bad that when he was given food to feed the pigs, he would eat some of it as that was all the food available.

As he sat with the pigs, his mind went back to his father's house. He thought about the wonderful life he had before, and how good things were before he left home.

He realized he made a foolish decision and the choice he made to demand his inheritance and leave home was not wise. He decided that he would return home to his father's house.

He knew he would have to ask his father to forgive him because he had disrespected him and made demands of him that were unreasonable and unfair.

He thought about the servants at the house and how they were doing better than he was.

Reason to Return

He prepared a speech that he would give to his father, and planned a date for return. He gathered the few things he had left and set out for his father's house.

When he left the house, he had an entourage and a motorcade. He was now walking back home lonely, broken, and destitute. He was not sure what to expect.

He knew he had to go home as this was his only chance for survival. Every other door was closed, and he ran out of options.

Meanwhile, back at the house where the father and older son resided, things were moving ahead, and business was good. The father was thinking about his younger son and even though he had left and not called or written after he left; the father was still hoping that he would return.

The older brother was not happy because since his brother left, a lot of the responsibilities for running the business fell to him and he did not have time to take a break or enjoy a vacation.

Earlier, he had heard news about his brother over in the city where he moved to. Someone messaged him to tell about the life his brother was living and he was furious.

One day as the father was in his chair on the porch taking his usual afternoon rest and relaxation, he looked down the road leading to the house and he saw someone walking in their direction.

He couldn't tell who it was but there was something familiar about the walk. As the person got nearer, he realized it was his son. He got up out of his chair, stretched and looked harder and confirmed it was his boy.

Reason to Celebrate

He felt compassion for him and took off running down the road, got to his son pulled him close, embraced him and kissed him.

The son was surprised and embarrassed as he never expected this kind of welcome. He started to tell his father the speech he had prepared about how he was not worthy to be his son and he should treat him as one of the servants.

The father was having none of this and called the servants to bring the fine robe he had ordered for this occasion and put it on him. He told them to put a ring on his hand and shoes on his feet.

He commanded the workers in the field to get the best calf, kill it and prepare it for a welcome feast for his son who had returned. He got them to schedule the band and invite the neighbors, for he was having a welcome home party.

The older brother was out in the field and as he came near to the house, he heard music and dancing. This was unusual because all that happened at the house lately, was work and business. He enquired from the servants what was going on. They told him his brother had returned and his father was having a celebration.

He was mad and refused to go in the house and join the party. His father came out and invited him in, but he replied to his father that he worked in the business for many years and was cooperative and compliant, yet he never had a party for him but now the rude, disrespectful, and ungrateful son who had wasted his fortune with prostitutes returned, he was celebrating.

The father responded that he will always be there for him and everything he owned belonged to him since the younger son already got his share.

It was fit to celebrate and rejoice, for his brother who was dead, is alive; he was lost, and is found. That's a real reason to give thanks and celebrate.

Chapter 14

A DIFFERENT WAY

There are some things that happen to us, and we have no logical explanation for how it happened. Likewise, there are people we meet, and we do not fully understand the connection until at some later time, it becomes clear.

The reasons for some things in life are hidden and is for a good reason. When the unexpected happens, we look back and say that it was good for us to have gone through the things we did.

No one enjoys pain or suffering, and we carefully avoid anything that would bring us hardship. The path to blessing is sometimes a painful journey.

Job was a good man. He was upright and honorable and earned the respect and love of those he associated with.

He was a family man and had a great relationship with his children. He looked out for them and made sure they were doing well.

To add to all his attributes, Job was a wealthy man. He owned property and many servants. If Job had been alive today, he would be considered a billionaire,

He was a kind and generous man and assisted those in need.

One day Satan and his angels came before God after being on a trip through the earth.

God asked Satan if he knew about Job and boasted about him. He talked about his character and righteous lifestyle. He said Job had a good heart and served God fearlessly.

Satan concluded the reason why Job lived the way he did was because God had built a hedge around him and protected him.

He challenged God that if He removed the hedge from around Job and exposed him to danger and calamity, he would become bitter and curse God.

That was a reasonable assumption as it is in keeping with human character. When things are going well, we are good and happy. However, when things take a different turn, we go sour and angry.

God took up Satan's challenge and decided to let him attack Job's property, riches, and family. He did not give him access to the man's body or his life.

Job was preparing for his workday after having breakfast and was about to make his usual rounds. There was a knock at the door and a messenger gave him a report that his herd of donkeys and oxen that were in the fields, were attacked and carried off by a band of robbers.

While the messenger was sharing the report of the robbery, another messenger showed up with a report about his sheep being burned up by fire and the shepherds were also killed in the blaze.

The messenger was telling his story, when another messenger came in and reported that his camels were raided by another gang of thieves and taken away with the servants who cared for them.

Before Job could sit down and absorb the messages that were coming in, there was another knock and another messenger with more bad news. This was about his children who were at a gathering at the brother's house and a storm came through the area and destroyed the house. His children were killed as the house collapsed.

In less than twenty-four hours, Job went from being a wealthy billionaire to losing his camels, cattle, donkeys, and children.

This was enough to send anyone over a cliff. It would have broken the ordinary person, but Job was a different man.

After hearing all the news, Job got up and tore his robe and shaved his head. He fell to the ground and declared that he had come into the world naked, and he would depart from the earth naked.

He acknowledged that it was God who gave him the things he had, and it was God who had the prerogative to take them away, He praised the name of the Lord.

Job never accused God of any wrong and he decided to be content with what was happening to him.

You would think that this would be the end of Job's suffering, but Satan approached God again regarding Job. He argued that even through all that had happened, he remained strong but if his body was attacked, it would break him, and he would give in.

God gave Satan permission to attack Job's body and he struck him with sores and boils that spread all over from his head to his toes. They were painful boils and caused him anguish.

While all of this was going on, Job's wife was observing from a distance. She finally approached him and suggested that he curse God and die. This would put him out of his misery.

Job replied that this was foolish advice because God had the authority to give and take away and He knew what was best for him. Job held strong and refused to curse God.

His friends came to visit him and comfort him. They began to discuss the matter of suffering and the things that their friend was experiencing. They concluded that bad things don't happen to good people and Job must have been involved in some secret sin and that he should confess and get well.

Job defended his integrity and called them miserable comforters. They came to offer support but were now accusing him of wrongdoing. After a series of arguments between the friends. Job concluded that he was innocent and was not involved in any evil.

God intervened in the dispute between Job and his friends and after reconciliation, Job prayed for them and God restored his fortune and gave him twice as much as he had before the disaster.

Job had to go through much testing and trials, but in the end, he came out triumphantly. There is a way to overcome, and God will always show the way.

Chapter 15

A DIFFERENT SPIRIT

After many years wandering in the wilderness, the Israelites were about to enter the land that was promised to them.

God instructed Moses to send men on a spy mission to Canaan to gather intelligence data. Moses selected twelve men who were leaders from each tribe to go on the mission.

The spies were given specific guidelines for the information they were to gather.

They were to check out the population of the city and see what the people was like, including their size and stature.

They would get soil samples and bring fruit from the trees to help them decide if the land was fertile.

They were going to check the security measures that were in place which would give them the best course of action to attack the city.

The men went throughout the land for forty days and returned with samples of grapes, pomegranates, and figs.

The spies came to an assembly with Moses, Aaron, and the Israelites to give a report. Ten of the men who had gone on the mission started off with the summary of the trip.

They showed them the fruit that they had brought back and described the land as one flowing with milk and honey. However, the people who dwell in the land were strong, and the cities were fortified and very large.

They continued their report by saying that there were giants in the land and the people were so tall and huge that when they were near to them, they seemed like grasshoppers.

The conclusion of the report was that because of the size and strength of the people, they were not able to go up against them for they were stronger and better equipped.

On hearing the negative report, the people panicked and started crying out against Moses and Aaron. They complained that they should have died in Egypt or in the wilderness and they would be in a better place had that happened.

They suggested that they choose new leaders who would take them back to Egypt.

Caleb and Joshua stood up and contradicted the report of the ten spies. They told the gathering that the land, which they went to spy out, was a good land and they were able to conquer it. They encouraged them to be calm and start planning to go in and occupy it because they could overcome it.

The people were in a very bad mood after hearing the previous men speak, they were in a state of defeat and discouragement, and they were not buying into Caleb and Joshua's story. They suggested that they should be stoned.

Ten men had instilled fear and doubt into the hearts and minds of the people and now that Caleb and Joshua were delivering a positive report, they could not see the possibilities and opportunities before them.

It took a lot of courage for these two men to stand up and share a message of hope when anxiety and uncertainty was already spreading through the congregation.

Very often, the negative voices are the loudest and the people who spread lies and bad information, can get their message across effectively.

When the voices of truth and reason is sounded, they get rejected and the people would rather listen to a message of doom and gloom than one of hope and victory.

Caleb and Joshua encouraged them to go in and possess the land. They saw the possibilities and knew that they had what it takes to do it successfully.

Most of the people who murmured and complained never got to see the land because of their unbelief. God promised that Caleb would enter the land because he had a different spirit.

What was the spirit he had? It was a bold and confident spirit. It was a spirit that affirmed that all things are possible to those who believe.

Chapter 16

MAKING A DIFFERENCE

One thing that a cook does constantly throughout the cooking process, is taste the food. This is to ensure that there is consistency, and they try to maintain the desired flavor of the recipe.

When the guests sit down to eat, it is the taste of the dish that will determine whether the food is good or not.

There are many different forms of spices that the cook uses to ensure good flavor. However, one of the most important seasonings is salt. This gives the dish a distinct taste and when it is added, it makes a difference in the recipe.

Salt is so important that it is placed in the water before the other ingredients are added. When the meal is served, a saltshaker is placed on the table so that it can be added to the meal if more is needed.

Jesus too realized the importance of salt. He saw a world in need of flavor and seasoning. He told the disciples in the Sermon on the Mount that they were the salt of the earth, and they would be added to help change and transform the world and bring zest and life to a place that was distasteful and bland.

In a world where there was no meaning, He decided to take these disciples who He had infused with his life-giving power and pour them out to make a difference.

The way that salt affects the dish is that it blends in with the other ingredients and touches them. The salt cannot remain on the counter or in the container and make a difference. It must come out of the can or bottle and get into the pot.

Salt maintains its flavor and does not taste like the other ingredients in the pot. They are in the same place and interact with each other as the pot boils. However, the salt does not end up tasting like the potato or the rice.

It is the exact opposite. The rice and all the other ingredients in the pot gets flavor from the salt.

Jesus made a very important point about the salt losing its saltiness. He said that if it lost its ability to make everything around it salty, then it was not good and had lost its effectiveness and should be thrown out.

Salt can be ineffective and lose its usefulness when it's been in the shaker or can for a while and either because of moisture, or lack of use, lumps are formed, and the holes in the container become clogged and the salt does not flow like it should.

There is a similar problem with church folks who should be the salt of the world. They gather in their bubble and remain closed and tight in their doctrines and belief systems. They lose their flow and the ability to connect and make a difference in their communities.

Chapter 17
DISPLAYING THE DIFFERENCE

Think about being in the middle of a storm where the sky is grey and dark, and during this already bleak situation, there is an electric power outage. Now there is darkness all around.

What makes this situation worst is that it is in the middle of the day when the sun should be shining, and all around should be light. Instead, it looks like night.

That is how it sometimes feel about the world we live in. With the money, innovations, and connectivity around us, it should be a place of warmth and light. Instead, it can be a cold and dark place.

No one enjoys living in the dark. It is uncomfortable and dangerous when you are in darkness. There is no awareness or understanding and bad things can happen.

We enjoy seeing the wonders of nature and enjoy beautiful scenery and just as plants need light to grow and develop, humans need light to thrive.

Jesus continued His sermon by declaring that we are the light of the world. When the darkness is prevailing, the people of light is turned on and makes a difference so that others may see the way clearly.

He talked about how it is not natural for a person to setup a lighting system and then cover it up. Instead, they would place the light in an open place where it would shine brightly and give light to everyone in the house.

This is how it should be with people of the heavenly kingdom. Their lights should shine brightly, and others would see their good deeds and as they observe the followers of Jesus living lives of excellence and distinction, they would give glory to God who is the Father, and the one who is the source of light.

He also made a reference to a city that was built on a hill. Because of its elevation, it stood out and it was evident to all and could be seen from a distance.

People who are different stand out and are on display. There are distinguishing marks by which they are identified and others around them see them clearly and are affected by their lives.

ABOUT THE AUTHOR

ROY BENJAMIN is an IT professional with over 25 years of experience in various areas of technology. He has worked as a consultant for various companies and provided tech support for many startups in Atlanta.

He is presently the Executive Director of Outreach Systems and offers consultation services for organizations, assisting in growth and development planning.

He served for many years in youth ministry and is a leader in men's outreach. As a speaker and thought leader, he has had opportunity to speak at many conferences and meetings around the world.

His time of service as a member of the Government of St. Kitts and Nevis has given him the experience and skills to work personally with leaders and people in top positions in other countries.

Roy is the author of Mission Vision Passion, a book about leadership lessons focused on the book of Nehemiah. He has shared these lessons with many individuals and groups.

He is available to speak at events and can be reached for consulting service at www.roybenjamin.net.

www.ingramcontent.com/pod-product-compliance
Lightning Source LLC
LaVergne TN
LVHW092058060526
838201LV00047B/1457